LIVING IN THE WILD: SEA MAMMALS

SEA OTTERS

Louise Spilsbury

Heinemann
LIBRARY
Chicago, Illinois

www.capstonepub.com
Visit our website to find out more information about Heinemann-Raintree books.

To order:

 Phone 800-747-4992

Visit www.capstonepub.com to browse our catalog and order online.

Edited by Adam Miller, Andrew Farrow, and Laura Knowles
Designed by Steve Mead
Picture research by Mica Brančić
Original illustrations © Capstone Global Library Ltd 2013
Illustrations by HL Studios
Originated by Capstone Global Library Ltd
Printed and bound in China by CTPS

16 15 14 13 12
10 9 8 7 6 5 4 3 2 1

Library of Congress Cataloging-in-Publication Data
Spilsbury, Louise.
  Sea otters / Louise Spilsbury.—1st ed.
    p. cm.—(Living in the wild: sea mammals)
  Includes bibliographical references and index.
  ISBN 978-1-4329-7065-9 (hb)—ISBN 978-1-4329-7072-7 (pb) 1.
Sea otter—Juvenile literature. I. Title.
  QL737.C25S686 2013
  599.769'5—dc23   2012013346

Acknowledgments
We would like to thank the following for permission to reproduce photographs: Alamy pp. 4 (© Malcolm Schuyl), 10 (© Alaska Stock/Bill Rome), 26 (© Rolf Hicker Photography), 32 (© Kevin Schafer), 33 (© Oleg Kozlov); Corbis pp. 13 (Minden Pictures/© Norbert Wu), 23 (Minden Pictures/© Sebastian Kennerknecht), 24 (Minden Pictures/© Suzi Eszterhas), 27 (Minden Pictures/© Michio Hoshino), 40 (© Karen Kasmauski); FLPA pp. 22 (Frans Lanting), 31 (Gerard Lacz); Getty Images pp. 14 (Minden Pictures/Kevin Schafer), 17 (National Geographic/Bates Littlehales), 18 (Discovery Channel Images/Jeff Foott), 20 (Oxford Scientific/David Courtenay), 21 (Minden Pictures/Donald M. Jones), 36 (Time Life Pictures/Stan Wayman), 43 (Minden Pictures/Donald M. Jones); Nature Picture Library pp. 7 (© Suzi Eszterhas), 11 (© Tom Mangelsen), 12 (© Doc White), 29 (© Matthew Maran), 34 (© Suzi Eszterhas), 45 (© Hans Christoph Kappel), Photoshot p. 38 (© Bruce Coleman/Mark Newman), Science Photo Library p. 30 (© Pat & Tom Leeson), Shutterstock pp. 15 (© Pyma), 16 (© vilainecrevette), 37(© Patsy Michaud).

Cover photograph of a Southern sea otter reproduced with permission of Corbis/© Hal Beral.

Every effort has been made to contact copyright holders of any material reproduced in this book. Any omissions will be rectified in subsequent printings if notice is given to the publisher.

Disclaimer
All the Internet addresses (URLs) given in this book were valid at the time of going to press. However, due to the dynamic nature of the Internet, some addresses may have changed, or sites may have changed or ceased to exist since publication. While the author and publisher regret any inconvenience this may cause readers, no responsibility for any such changes can be accepted by either the author or the publisher.

Contents

Some words are shown in bold, **like this**. You can find out what they mean by looking in the glossary.

What Are Sea Mammals?

A dark shape appears below the surface of the sea. A moment later, there is a splash, and then a furry, round head peeks above the water. It is a sea otter, one of the many **mammals** that live or spend most of their lives in the sea.

Sea mammals are animals that need the sea for food and spend most of their time in or near the sea. Like land mammals, sea mammals give birth to live young, and the mothers feed their babies milk. They also have backbones and hair on their bodies, although on many sea mammals, this hair is barely visible.

Sea otters are the smallest sea mammals in the world. They weigh between 35 and 90 pounds (16 and 40 kilograms).

Common features

There are around 130 different types, or **species**, of sea mammal. They have adapted in different ways to live in the sea. Some, such as whales and dolphins, spend their whole lives in the water. Others, such as seals and sea lions, feed in the ocean but regularly **haul out** onto land to breed or rest. Like land mammals, all sea mammals need to breathe air. They can hold their breath for a longer time as they dive underwater in search of food, but they always come back to the surface to breathe. They also have thick fat (blubber) or fur to stay warm in cold water.

Type of sea mammal	How do they move?	Where do they live?
Whales and dolphins	use tail, fins, and flippers	These sea mammals live in water all the time.
Manatees and dugongs	use tail and flippers	
Seals, sea lions, and walruses	use flippers	These sea mammals spend some of their time in water and some on land.
Sea otters	use legs and tail	
Polar bears	use legs	

Sea otters and polar bears are grouped together because both have paws instead of flippers or fins like other sea mammals.

What Are Sea Otters?

Sea otters are mammals with brown fur, a slender body, short legs, and a long, muscular tail. There are 13 species, or types, of otter in the world. Most live mainly in freshwater rivers, but two species almost always live in salty seawater. The marine otter lives along the Pacific coast of South America, partly on the rocky seashore and partly in the water. The sea otter rarely leaves the ocean and is the only otter species to give birth in the water.

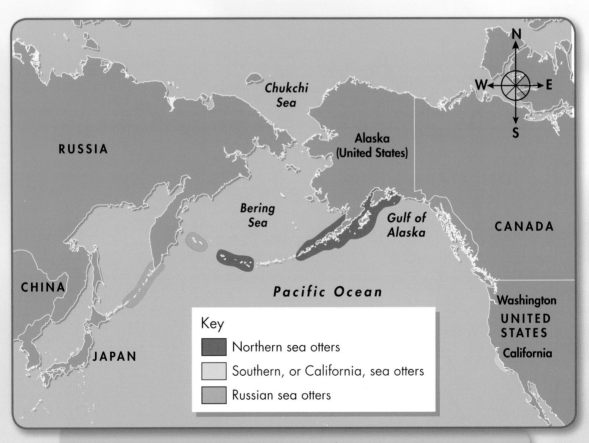

Key
- Northern sea otters
- Southern, or California, sea otters
- Russian sea otters

Sea otters are only found in the North Pacific Ocean. Around 90 percent of the world's sea otters are Northern sea otters living in the waters around Alaska.

Sea otter evolution

Sea otters probably **evolved** about 5 to 7 million years ago. Their ancestors may have been land mammals that started to hunt in the sea because there was more food there than along the coast. They may also have wanted to escape animals that hunted them on land. Gradually, these ancient otters developed **adaptations** that helped them live an ocean life. An adaptation is a feature that allows an animal to live in a particular place in a particular way. Animals develop adaptations as species evolve over thousands of years.

GEORG WILHELM STELLER

In 1741, German scientist Georg Wilhelm Steller was shipwrecked on the **uninhabited** Commander Islands between Alaska and eastern Russia. He realized that no one had ever described or written about the mammals he saw in the waters there. Steller named them sea otters.

Sea otters move clumsily on land and rarely come out of the water, unlike other otters, which can move easily on land.

How Are Sea Otters Classified?

Scientists **classify** living things to identify them and to understand why and how they live where they do. *Classification* means grouping living things according to the characteristics or features they share.

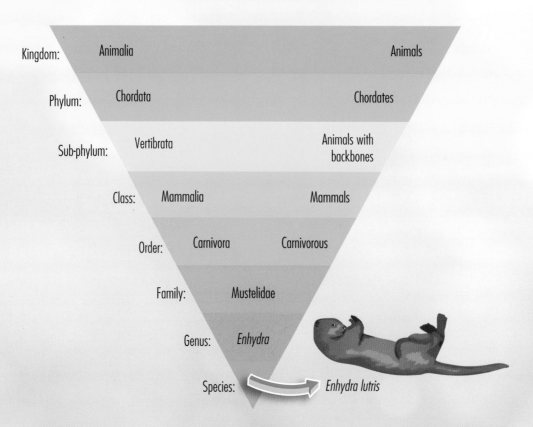

Kingdom:	Animalia	Animals
Phylum:	Chordata	Chordates
Sub-phylum:	Vertibrata	Animals with backbones
Class:	Mammalia	Mammals
Order:	Carnivora	Carnivorous
Family:	Mustelidae	
Genus:	*Enhydra*	
Species:		*Enhydra lutris*

This pyramid shows how the sea otter is classified. The scientific name *Enhydra lutris* means "otter that lives in the water."

Classification groups

A classification triangle shows how a living thing is classified. Each group contains fewer and fewer members. So, there are fewer animals in the class Mammalia (mammals) than in the sub-phylum Vertebrata (animals with backbones), and so on. Sea otters are in the family Mustelidae, which includes weasel-like carnivores (meat-eaters) with long, slender bodies. Sea otters are the smallest sea mammal, but they are the heaviest animals in the Mustelid family.

Sea otter subspecies

Living things are given a Latin name, such as *Enhydra lutris*, to avoid confusion if they are known by different common names in different countries. Sometimes living things are classified into groups within species because of slight differences between them, such as where they live or their size.

There are three subspecies of sea otter found in different parts of the Pacific Ocean: Southern (or California), Northern, and Russian sea otters. You can find the areas where they live on the map on page 6. All types of sea otter look similar and live very similar lives, but the Russian sea otter is generally bigger than the other two.

Subspecies	Latin name	Distribution
Northern sea otter	*Enhydra lutris kenyoni*	Washington state, Alaska, and Canada
Southern, or California, sea otter	*Enhydra lutris nereis*	California
Russian sea otter	*Enhydra lutris lutris*	Russia and Japan

Where Do Sea Otters Live?

An animal's **habitat** is the place where it lives. A habitat provides an animal with everything it needs, including food, water, and shelter. The sea otter's habitat is seawater, usually within about half a mile (1 kilometer) of the coast.

Coastal habitats

Sea otters stay near the shore, where the water does not get deeper than 100 feet (30 meters). That is because they get food from the sea floor, and they can only dive so deep on a single breath of air. They usually choose coastlines that give them some protection from strong waves, such as rocky **reefs** and thick **kelp** forests. Sea otters around Alaska can live where there is some ice drifting in the water, but not farther north, where solid ice covers the sea.

Sea otters around Alaska may haul out onto ice to rest during harsh winters.

Sea otters live in cold seas. They often wrap themselves in kelp and hold their feet out of the chilly water. Then their feet can absorb warmth from the sun!

Among the kelp forests

Kelp is large seaweed that grows in colder seas. It can be up to 130 feet (40 meters) tall! It has large, root-like holdfasts that attach to the ocean floor and long, branching stalks that float to the surface. Kelp forests form rich habitats that are home to many **invertebrates** and fish, as well as the sea otter. Sea otters spend most of their time in kelp forests off the west coast of North America, Alaska, and Russia. The southernmost point of their habitat is where kelp forests end. Individual sea otters usually stay in a **home range** a few miles long.

What Adaptations Help Sea Otters Survive?

The sea otter has many adaptations that help it survive in the cold sea. Its back feet are adapted for swimming. They are broad, **webbed**, and powerful. The sea otter uses them like flippers to propel it through the water.

The tail is also strong. When the sea otter is floating on its back, it moves around by using its back legs and twisting its tail from side to side. Sea otters usually swim at speeds of up to 1¼ miles per hour (2 kilometers per hour). By bending their body and tail up and down, they can swim as fast as 5 miles per hour (8 kilometers per hour) for short bursts underwater.

Sea otter nostrils and ears close underwater. They can also change the shape of the **lenses** in their eyes to help them see underwater.

Diving deep

Sea mammals have to come to the surface to breathe air, but sea otters can hold their breath for up to five minutes underwater. The sea otter's lungs are two-and-a-half times bigger than other mammals the same size, so they can stay underwater longer finding food. Having large lungs that hold lots of air also keeps sea otters **buoyant**, helping them to swim back up after diving or to float on the surface.

Sea otters have a larger chest than other otters because their rib cage needs to cover and protect their big lungs.

Keeping warm

How can a sea otter stay warm in freezing-cold seawater? Its body is covered with a double layer of fur. There is a **dense**, soft layer of fur next to the skin. This traps a layer of warm air over the skin that keeps their body temperature at around 100 degrees Fahrenheit (38 degrees Celsius). There is a layer of long, thin hairs on top of this underfur to form a waterproof outer coat. This is very important, because the fur underneath cannot trap heat when it gets wet.

Sea otters have the densest fur of any mammal. A sea otter has around 1 million hairs on every square inch (6 square centimeters) of its body—nearly 10 times as much as on your whole head!

Getting bubbles of air into their fur helps sea otters float.

Making heat

To help it stay warm in cold water, a sea otter has a **metabolic rate** twice as high as other otters. That means its body converts food into energy twice as quickly. To fuel its fast metabolism, a sea otter needs to eat up to a quarter of its body weight every day. That is like a 10-year-old child who weighs 79 pounds (36 kilograms) eating more than 80 quarter-pound hamburgers every day!

HAIRY FLOATS

The sea otter's dense fur also makes it more buoyant and helps it to float because the fur traps large amounts of air. Sea otters know how to trap more air inside their fur, too! They roll at the surface of the water and even blow bubbles of air around the base of the hairs when they **groom** (clean) their fur.

What Do Sea Otters Eat?

Sea otters are **predators**. They eat animals they find or catch in the sea. They eat many kinds of invertebrates, although Alaska sea otters also eat fish sometimes. Sea otters eat around 40 different types of invertebrate, including abalone, snails, starfish, sea urchins, crabs, clams, mussels, squid, and octopus. However, individual sea otters have favorite foods and often eat only two to four of these. This might explain why so many sea otters can share one particular habitat.

PURPLE BONES!

When sea otter bones wash ashore, some have a slight purple tinge! That is evidence that those sea otters had eaten lots of sea urchins. Sea urchins contain a natural purple coloring that moves into the otters' bones.

Sea otters find food on the sea floor below the surface of the water, where they rest.

Hunting

Sea otters can see well underwater, but the water they hunt in is often dark or murky, so they often use their sense of touch. They use their front paws to feel along the sea floor for food. They use their long whiskers to feel vibrations in the water caused by the movements of **prey**.

A sea otter's front paws have rough pads and claws. These help it dig for and grab prey and twist or pull it off rocks. Sea otters usually dive for about a minute at a time. They often dive several times before capturing prey. Then they tuck it into a loose pouch of skin under their front leg to carry it to the surface.

A sea otter's long whiskers help it to locate and identify prey.

Feeding

When sea otters bring food to the surface, they lie on their backs and use their stomach as a table. Sea otters swallow some small prey whole, such as fish. They twist large shells apart with their paws and claws and scrape out the meat from inside with their sharp front teeth. Their large, flat back teeth crush and grind food. They avoid being hurt by a sea urchin's spines by rubbing them off with their paws or biting through the base, where spines are shorter, and licking out the flesh.

A SALTY DRINK

Sea otters get most of the water they need from their food, but they also drink seawater to quench their thirst. The salt in seawater would kill most mammals. Like some other sea mammals, a sea otter's large kidneys remove the salt and get rid of it in the animal's urine.

Sea otters rest wriggling prey on their stomachs and eat it quickly, before the animals get away!

Sea otter food web

Animals eat other animals or plants and, in turn, may be eaten by other animals. This sequence is called a **food chain**. An ocean food chain starts with **algae**, such as seaweed, which make their own food using energy from sunlight. They are called producers. Animals are called consumers because they consume (eat) other animals or plants. Many connected food chains make up a **food web**. In this food web, for example, sea urchins and abalone eat kelp. Sea otters eat sea urchins, abalone, and the starfish that eat abalone, too.

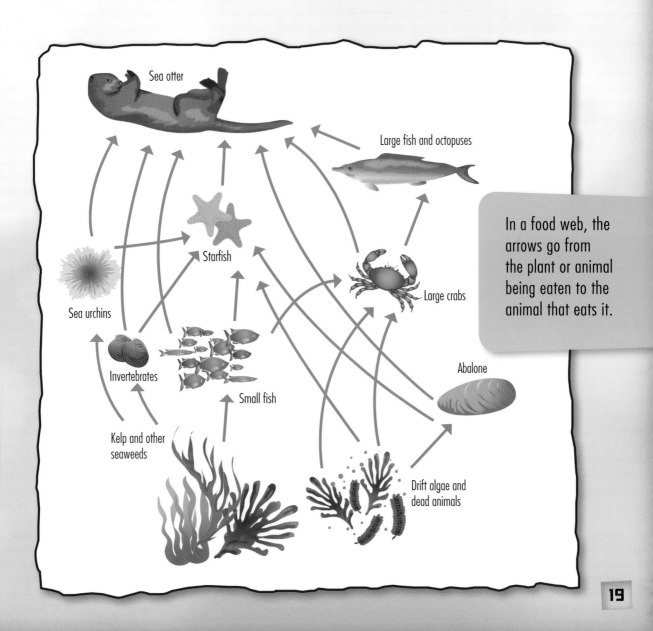

Sea otter

Large fish and octopuses

Starfish

Sea urchins

Large crabs

Invertebrates

Abalone

Small fish

Kelp and other seaweeds

Drift algae and dead animals

In a food web, the arrows go from the plant or animal being eaten to the animal that eats it.

What Is a Sea Otter's Life Cycle?

An animal's life cycle is the stages it goes through from birth to death. Sea mammals go through three main stages: birth, youth, and adulthood. Adulthood is when they reproduce and have young themselves.

Meeting and mating

Adult male and female sea otters usually live in different parts of a coastline. They only come together to **mate**. Males mate with more than one female, but females mate with only one male. This makes them rather fussy about whom they mate with. A female gives off a scent to show she is ready to mate, but if she does not like the male that this scent attracts, she pushes him away. After mating with a suitable male, the pair separates, and the female gives birth to a pup about six months later.

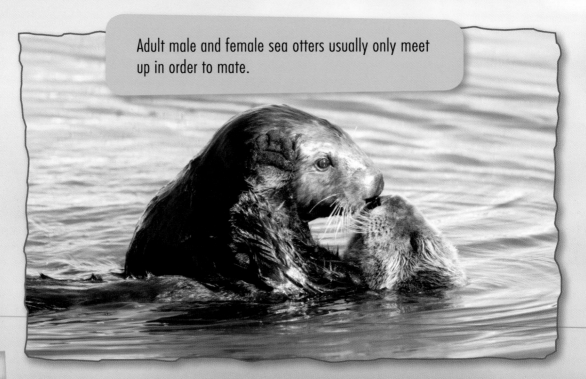

Adult male and female sea otters usually only meet up in order to mate.

A pup is born

Females give birth to a single pup in the water. A female rolls around in the water, and then she suddenly appears holding a wet, fluffy pup in her teeth. Sea otters can be born throughout the year, but most pups in Alaska are born in May and June, and in California more are born between January and March.

Sea otter pups are between 22 to 24 inches (56 and 61 centimeters) long and weigh 4.5 to 5 pounds (2 to 2.3 kilograms).

Pup development

When sea otter pups are born, they have open eyes and a set of small teeth. A sea otter mother cares for her newborn pup by herself. Like other mammals, she feeds her young on milk from her body. Sea otter milk contains up to 25 percent fat, so pups grow fast on this rich milk.

A sea otter pup **suckles** while its mother floats on her back.

Protective mothers

A sea otter mother is very protective of her pup. She constantly grooms its coat to ensure the fur keeps the pup warm and helps it to float. If a sea otter mother spots danger, she grabs the pup by the scruff of the neck with her teeth and swims out of sight.

A sea otter mother lays the pup on her stomach while she floats on the surface, to stop it from freezing by being in the cold water too long.

Wrapped in kelp

The only time a mother leaves her pup floating alone on the water is when she dives for food. Before doing so, she wraps the pup in kelp, to stop it from drifting away. Being draped in kelp also hides the pup from any predators that might pass by while its mother is not there.

MICHELLE STAEDLER

Scientist Michelle Staedler studies sea otter pups in the wild to know how to care for pups that are separated from their mothers. By understanding what pups need, she can tell helpers in sea otter centers how to care for rescued pups. She learns when to teach pups the skills they will need to survive after they are released back into the wild.

Life lessons

A sea otter mother carries her pup on her chest until it is about two months old. Then the pup learns to swim and dive. A pup learns by watching its mother, who stays close so that the pup can get back onto her belly when it is tired.

Sea otters suckle from their mothers for six to eight months, but after about four weeks, the mother shares pieces of prey with them, too. Pups follow her to learn how to hunt once they can dive to the sea floor. The reason different sea otters have different hunting skills and eat different prey is because they learn different hunting skills from their mothers.

Pups remain dependent on their mothers for at least six months, and in that time she teaches them how to dive and hunt and what to eat.

The cycle begins again...

At around eight months to one year old, young sea otters are ready to leave their mothers. A young male may travel hundreds of miles to find a new feeding area. Female sea otters become adults and can have their own young from about four years old. Males are capable of mating at five or six, but they do not usually start to mate with females for several more years. A female gives birth roughly every one to two years, depending on how long her previous pup stays with her. When these pups grow up, the whole cycle begins again.

PUP SURVIVAL

Mothers must groom their pups' fur until the pups learn to do it themselves. If fur is not groomed, it does not keep out the cold water. Sea otter pups separated from their mothers die within hours from cold and lack of food.

This chart shows the life span of some sea mammals in the wild. Male sea otters live an average of 10 to 15 years, while female sea otters live an average of 15 to 20 years.

Sea mammal	Life span
Leopard seal	12–15 years
Sea otter	15–23 years
Harbor porpoise	average 20 years
California sea lion	up to 30 years
Walrus	up to 40 years
Beluga whale	35–50 years
Blue whale	80–90 years

Source: *National Geographic*

How Do Sea Otters Behave?

Sea otters mostly live alone, but they sometimes gather in groups when resting. These groups of floating sea otters are known as rafts.

Individuals in a raft take turns acting as guards. They swim at the edge of the raft and watch out for predators.

Females and their young pups form separate rafts from adult males, and the rafts vary in size. Rafts in California tend to contain around 12 otters, but they can include up to 50 animals. In Alaska, where most sea otters live, there can be several hundred animals in a raft. People have even spotted rafts of 2,000 sea otters! Sea otters in a raft sometimes hold onto each other's paws to stay together.

This large raft of sea otters lives in the sea near Alaska.

Patrolling a territory

Males and females only come together to mate. At mating time, males do not form rafts—instead, each male sets up his own **territory**. A territory is an area that an animal guards as its own. A male sea otter swims around and patrols his territory. He might hiss or lunge at other males who enter it, to keep them away. However, he may approach and mate with a female who enters the territory—if she accepts him. Sometimes a male sets up a territory that already includes a raft of females. Males and females stay together for about three days during mating. Then the female swims off and the male continues to patrol his territory, watching out for other females.

A DAY IN THE LIFE OF A SEA OTTER

Sea otters are busy during the daytime and sleep at night. During the day, they eat and groom a lot, but they also rest at the water's surface for long stretches of time.

HUNTING AND FEEDING

As soon as sea otters wake up in the morning, they start to hunt and feed. After a rest at midday, they feed for a few hours more in the afternoon. Mothers with pups may also wake to feed in the night, because it is safer to leave pups alone then. The amount of time a sea otter spends hunting depends on how much food is available. In places where there are many sea otters or food is scarce, hunting takes longer.

How does an otter spend its time?

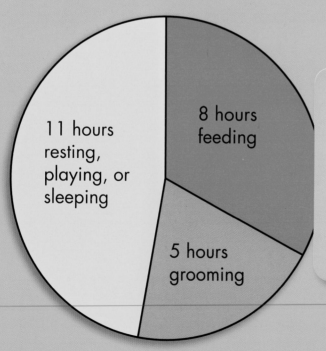

11 hours resting, playing, or sleeping

8 hours feeding

5 hours grooming

In an average 24-hour day, a sea otter spends about 8 hours feeding, 5 to 6 hours grooming, and about 10 or 11 hours resting, playing, or sleeping.

A sea otter licks its coat and uses its paws and claws to remove dirt and to comb its fur.

GROOMING AND PLAYING

Sea otters spend between one third and one half of their waking hours grooming. Grooming is very important, because outer fur is less waterproof when it is dirty or matted. Then the underfur gets wet and sea otters get cold. Pups and adults also play. They chase and explore things floating in the sea and tumble around with each other.

TIME FOR BED!

Sea otters mostly sleep at sea, often in rafts, floating on their backs on the surface. They roll over and over to wrap their bodies in kelp so that they do not drift away while they sleep. Some sea otters in Alaska haul out onto land and sleep huddled together for warmth.

How Intelligent Are Sea Otters?

It is very difficult to measure and compare intelligence in animals, but scientists think that sea otters are as intelligent and able to learn as dogs. They are inquisitive, communicate in different ways, and even use tools, unlike most other animals.

Using tools

Sea otters eat many animals that are protected by hard shells, so they use tools to open them. A sea otter lies on its back, rests a stone on its stomach, and hits a shell against the stone to break it open. Then it can eat the animal inside. Some sea otters find any nearby stone to use, but many have a favorite stone that they carry with them, tucked into an underarm pouch.

When sea otters find a stone that is a good one for breaking open shells, they carry it with them at all times!

Stone hammers

Sea otters also use their stone tools to knock prey off rocks. Abalones, for example, have hard and heavy shells and can suck onto rocks with tremendous force. To get an abalone off its rock, a sea otter hammers the shell with a stone. It may have to dive several times before finally knocking the abalone off the rock with its stone.

BOAT BASHING

In places where sea otters live near people, they have learned a new technique for opening shells. They smash the shells against the side of a boat and even figure out where the boat is hardest and best for cracking. They have cleverly taken a skill learned from their mother and adjusted it to new surroundings.

A sea otter may dive down with its tool many times to get large prey.

Communication

Communication is another sign of intelligence in sea otters. It shows they can understand what is going on around them and share that information with others. A baby sea otter cries when it is left alone. It makes a shrill "weee" sound, similar to a seagull's cry. This loud scream can be heard for miles, so a mother can find her lost pup if it drifts off while she is hunting.

Most sea otter sounds cannot be heard from the shore, but people sometimes hear pups' noisy calls.

Rubbing noses together is one friendly way that sea otters communicate with each other.

Adult sounds

Sea otters mainly make sounds above rather than under the water. They often whistle or whine to show anger and frustration. They hiss or growl to warn predators to back off and may whistle or scream when frightened. Sea otters make grunting sounds when they are enjoying a meal, and females make gentle, cooing sounds to express contentment when they are grooming their pup's fur.

Body language

Sea otters also communicate using body language. Moving their heads from side to side is like saying hello. They also rub their faces together and touch noses. This is a way of recognizing each other by scent and showing each other they are friendly.

What Threats Do Sea Otters Face?

Today, the International Union for **Conservation** of Nature and Natural Resources (IUCN) lists the sea otter as an **endangered** species. This means there is a serious risk that all the animals from the species will die.

Human hunters

The main reason sea otters are endangered today is because of hunting in the past. Russians began hunting sea otters for their fur in 1741. They were soon joined by British and American hunters. Sea otter numbers dropped from around 300,000 in the 1700s to less than 2,000 by 1911, when the sea otter fur trade was stopped. After 1911, sea otter numbers gradually increased. However, since the 1990s, numbers have been dropping again.

The trade in sea otter fur began after Georg Steller and other survivors (see page 7) returned with sea otter skins.

Predators

Most sea otters hear predators coming and escape by diving fast or hiding among kelp. Great white sharks catch some sea otters in California, while orcas (or killer whales) have reduced sea otter numbers in Alaska. Land predators such as coyotes, bears, and eagles may also eat pups and weaker sea otters in Alaska.

JAMES ESTES

In the 1990s, biologist James Estes used radio collars to track two groups of sea otters around the Aleutian Islands in Alaska. Numbers fell in the group that orcas could reach. Orcas used to mostly eat Steller sea lions and harbor seals, but these sea mammals are dying because fishermen take the fish they eat. Estes realized orcas were hunting sea otters instead.

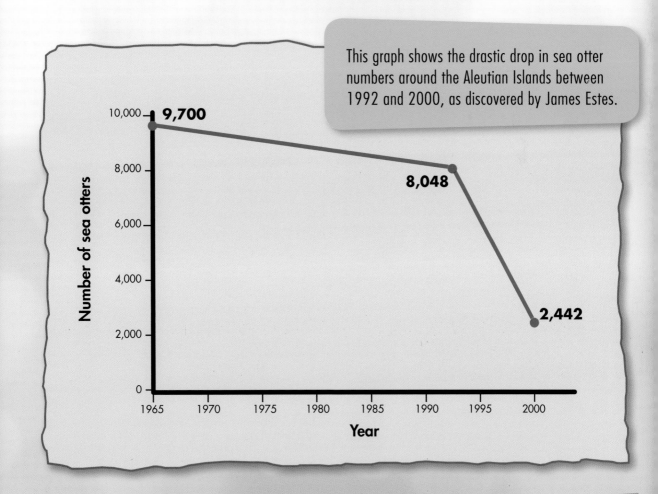

This graph shows the drastic drop in sea otter numbers around the Aleutian Islands between 1992 and 2000, as discovered by James Estes.

Pollution

Pollution is another threat to sea otters today. Pollution is when something that has harmful or poisonous effects gets into water, air, or land. Oil spills at sea clog fur, so sea otters freeze. Licking oily fur or eating oiled prey damages organs inside the sea otter's body. Other types of pollution, such as human waste and farm chemicals washed off land, get into a sea otter's body from the water or through the prey that the otter eats. This builds up and weakens the sea otter's body and makes it more likely to catch diseases or to be killed by infections.

In 1989, oil spilled from the wrecked tanker *Exxon Valdez* killed up to 10,000 otters off Alaska. Oil on a sea otter's fur is so dangerous that some scientists fear that a major oil spill could kill many or all of the world's sea otters.

Boats can damage kelp forests and harm sea otters. One-fifth of sea otter deaths are caused by accidents, such as being hit by a boat. Some sea otters drown when they become tangled in boats' fishing nets.

Habitat loss

Sea otters are also threatened by habitat loss. Some kelp plants are damaged by boat propellers and fishing gear when ships travel over kelp forests. Kelp is harvested for algin, a substance used to make products like ice cream, salad dressings, and toothpastes smooth and creamy. When too much kelp is harvested from one area or cut too regularly, it will not grow back. Water pollution can also harm kelp habitats by stopping young kelp plants from growing properly.

How Can People Help Sea Otters?

Many people are working to help these endangered sea mammals. Although sea otters have some protection from laws in the United States, Canada, and Russia, more needs to be done. Conservation groups press governments to increase their protection—for example, by increasing fines and penalties for people who harm sea otters and by improving regulations about waste and pollution released into the sea. California sea otters live in areas at risk of oil spills from passing oil tankers and oil rigs, so the conservation group Ocean Conservancy is pushing for traffic lanes for tankers well off the California coast, to reduce oil spill threats.

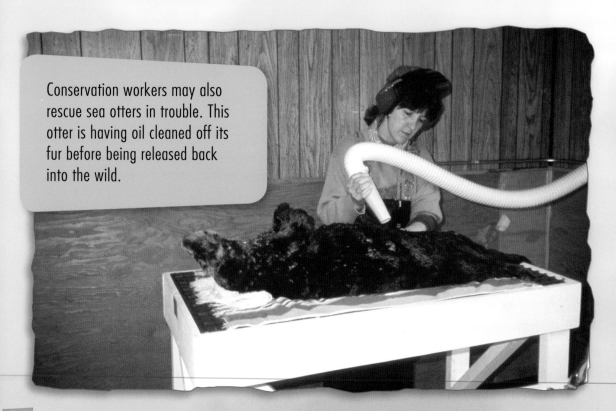

Conservation workers may also rescue sea otters in trouble. This otter is having oil cleaned off its fur before being released back into the wild.

Parks and sanctuaries

Governments and conservation groups also help sea otters by setting up parks and sanctuaries. For example, the U.S. government set up the Monterey Bay National Marine Sanctuary in California in 1992. Activities such as dumping waste and drilling for oil are banned in this protected area of water, and scientists can study the sea otters that live there. Parks and aquariums may also rescue orphaned, sick, and injured sea otters and help them to recover. They can also help people to appreciate sea otters and understand what needs to be done to protect them.

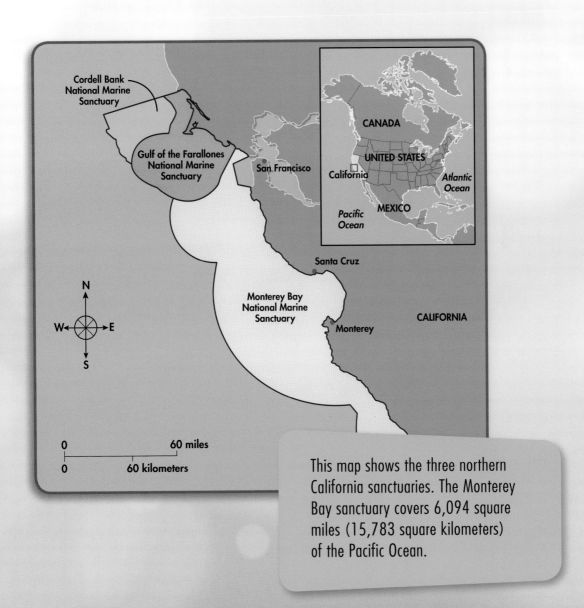

This map shows the three northern California sanctuaries. The Monterey Bay sanctuary covers 6,094 square miles (15,783 square kilometers) of the Pacific Ocean.

Research

Research is very important to help sea otters. For example, we know numbers are declining because teams of scientists use binoculars and telescopes to count sea otters from the coast and from airplanes. Scientists also study changes in sea otter habitats and water quality to help them understand what makes populations decline. Then they can advise governments and conservation groups on how to help sea otters.

KATHERINE RALLS

Scientist Katherine Ralls is studying sea otters in California. She attaches radio transmitters to sea otters. These send her information about the otters' daily lives, such as their body temperature and how long and where they dive for food. By comparing this information to a similar study in the 1990s, she hopes to find out more about why California sea otter numbers are declining.

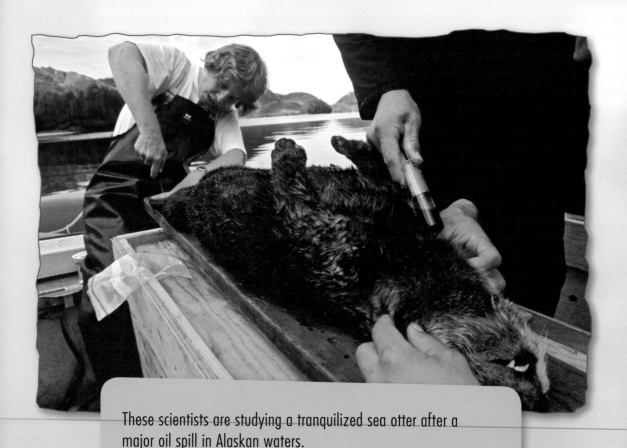

These scientists are studying a tranquilized sea otter after a major oil spill in Alaskan waters.

What can you do?

People can help sea otters by reducing the waste substances that end up in the sea and reducing the amount of oil they use. Here are some ways you can help:

- Use paper bags rather than plastic and Styrofoam packages that are made with oil.

- Share car trips, ride a bike, or take a bus to reduce oil use.

- Buy local foods and products that use less gasoline for deliveries.

- Fix oil leaks and dispose of used oil properly.

- Use vegetable- or fruit-based detergents (rather than oil-based detergents) around the house.

- Reduce the amount of harmful chemicals your family pours down sinks.

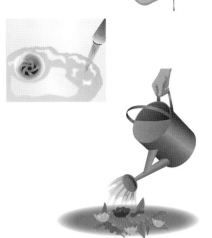

- Encourage your family to use nontoxic weedkillers and other garden products.

What Does the Future Hold for Sea Otters?

The future for sea otters does not look good unless pollution, overfishing, and habitat destruction are all controlled or stopped. In the future, **global warming** may also be a threat, as this is gradually increasing the temperature of the oceans. As kelp forests only grow in cold water, a rise in temperature could further reduce the sea otter's kelp forest habitat.

Interdependence

Interdependence is the way the living things in a habitat and the habitat itself rely on each other for survival. The sea otter is a **keystone species**, which means that dramatic changes happen to its habitat if it is removed. When sea otters were almost wiped out by the fur trade, sea urchins greatly increased in number because there were few sea otters to eat them. The sea urchins ate so much kelp that many kelp habitats were destroyed. After the ban on hunting, the sea otter populations grew again—and so did the kelp forests and the 800 other species that depend on the kelp forests for survival.

Hope for the future

Many organizations, individuals, and governments are working to protect sea otters. Captive breeding programs may also help. This is when animals are born and raised in zoos. Scientists study sea otters in a zoo to get a better understanding of their needs and how to protect them in the wild. They may also release them into the wild. We can only hope that actions people take today will save these fascinating creatures for the future.

It is important that sea otters survive in the future—for the health of other sea life and their ocean habitats, and to enrich the natural world for us all.

Species Profile

Species: Sea otter

Latin name: *Enhydra lutris*

Length: Up to 65 inches (160 centimeters)

Weight: Up to 90 pounds (40 kilograms)

Habitat: Kelp forests in the ocean

Diet: Invertebrates such as clams, sea urchins, crabs, and snails

Number of young: One infant is born after around six months of pregnancy. Females will give birth about every one to two years.

Life expectancy: Average of 10 to 15 years for males; 15 to 20 years for females

fur—dense, double layer of hair for warmth and buoyancy

tail—flattened for pushing through the water and steering

eye—can see above and below water

back feet—flattened and flipper-like

whiskers—can feel tiny vibrations in the water

front feet—sensitive paws for feeling with pads and claws for gripping

Glossary

adaptation body part or behavior of a living thing that helps it survive in a particular habitat

algae plant-like living thing that grows on land and in the sea

classify group living things together by their similarities and differences

buoyant able to float

conservation protection or restoration of wildlife and the natural environment

dense packed closely together

endangered describes a species that is in danger of dying out

evolve change gradually over time

food chain sequence in which one creature eats another, which eats another, and so on

food web network of intertwined food chains

global warming rise in the temperature of Earth's atmosphere

groom clean an animal's fur

habitat type of place or surroundings that a living thing prefers to live in

haul out leave the water to get on land

home range area in which an animal usually lives

interdependence way that all of the living things in a habitat and the habitat itself rely on each other for survival

invertebrate animal that does not have a backbone

kelp type of large, brown seaweed

keystone species type of living thing that is important for the survival of its habitat and the other living things in it

lens part of an animal's eye that gathers light

mammal animal that has fur or hair, gives birth to live young, and feeds its young on milk from the mother

mate come together to reproduce or have young

metabolic rate amount of energy an animal uses just to stay alive

oxygen gas in the air that animals need to breathe

pollution something that gets into the environment and has harmful or poisonous effects

predator animal that hunts and kills another animal for food

prey animal that is hunted and killed for food by another animal

reef hard ridge of rock or coral that is underwater, but near the surface

species group of similar living things that can mate with each other

suckle take milk from a mother's body

territory area of land that an animal claims as its own

uninhabited not lived in by humans

webbed having skin between toes or fingers

Find Out More

Books

Lockwood, Sophie. *Sea Otters* (World of Mammals). Chanhassen, Minn.: Child's World, 2006.

Slade, Suzanne. *What If There Were No Sea Otters?* (Food Chain Reactions). Mankato, Minn.: Picture Window Books, 2011.

Stefoff, Rebecca. *Sea Mammals* (Family Trees). New York: Marshall Cavendish Children's Books, 2009.

Web sites

animals.nationalgeographic.com/animals/mammals/sea-otter
Learn more about sea otters at this National Geographic web site.

www.montereybayaquarium.org/animals/default.aspx?c=dd
Type "sea otter" into the search engine of the Animal Guide section of this web site to find out more about sea otters and their conservation.

www.seaworld.org/animal-info/info-books/otters/
You will find lots of information about all types of otters on the Seaworld web site.

Organizations to contact

Friends of the Sea Otter
www.seaotters.org
This organization focuses on saving sea otters.

The Otter Project
www.otterproject.org
This organization is actively working to keep sea otters from dying out.

WWF
www.worldwildlife.org
WWF works to protect animals and nature and needs your help! Take a look at its web site and see what you can do.

Index